# Visiting a
# SYNAGOGUE

# Visiting a
# SYNAGOGUE

## Douglas Charing

**Photography**
**MELVYN NEWMAN**

**Illustration/Design**
**JUDY BILLSON**

LUTTERWORTH PRESS
CAMBRIDGE

Lutterworth Press
P.O. Box 60
Cambridge CB1 2NT

*British Library Cataloguing in Publication Data available*

First published in UK 1984 by Lutterworth Press
Reprinted 1988

The author extends his most grateful thanks to Rabbi Reuven Silverman, Mr Norman Franks, the General Secretary and the Executive and Council of the Jackson's Row Synagogue for their unstinting assistance in compiling this book.

When you look up the passages from the Bible remember that the first number after the name of the book is the chapter number, and the other numbers refer to the verses; so, Leviticus 14:5–11 is the Book of Leviticus, chapter 14, verses 5 to 11. If the verse numbers are written 5, 11 it means verses 5 and 11.

ISBN 0-7188-2573-X

Printed in Great Britain by
St Edmundsbury Press Limited, Bury St Edmunds, Suffolk

# Contents

# 1. Visiting a Synagogue

What is a synagogue? It is a meeting place where Jews gather to pray, to study the Torah, the word of God, and to make contact with their friends.

Jews have been meeting in synagogues for many centuries in many lands. This book is about one of the synagogues in Britain, the Manchester Reform Synagogue. It is also known as Jackson's Row Synagogue and this is the name we shall use.

## WHO ARE THE JEWS?

The Jews are a very ancient people. Abraham, their forefather, lived nearly 4,000 years ago. They think of him as the first Jew. Other famous Jews include Moses and King David. Although the Jewish people originally lived in Israel, they were great travellers and can now be found in most countries of the world. In Britain, most Jewish people live in the London area but a large number also live in other major cities such as Manchester, Leeds and Glasgow.

## THE JEWISH COMMUNITY IN BRITAIN

Jews first came to Britain in the days of William the Conqueror. They began to settle there but often they were badly treated and in 1290 King Edward I expelled them. In 1656 Jewish families began to return to Britain, mainly from Holland. In later centuries too Jews came to Britain, many escaping from persecution in Eastern Europe.

## JEWS IN MANCHESTER

The Jewish community in Manchester is not very old but it is one of the largest in the country. It was founded in the 1780s by two brothers from Liverpool. The first Jewish place of worship was

*The Old Manchester Reform Synagogue*

built in 1804 though the original cemetery in St Thomas' Church is ten years older. The first spiritual leader was a rabbi from Hungary, Joseph Crool.

As the Jews settled, many began to work in the clothing industry. Some helped to make new material whilst others were tailors. In 1870 there were about 5,000 Jews in Manchester and just twenty years later 20,000. At present the Jewish population is 35,000. Over the years it has included famous people, notably Dr Chaim Weitzmann, the first president of the State of Israel.

# 2. What is a Synagogue?

There have been synagogues for over two thousand years. Like churches and other places of worship, they come in all shapes and sizes. In Britain you can find old synagogues built in the 19th century and also new modern buildings put up in the present day. The Jackson's Row Synagogue dates from the 1950s although an earlier building existed for many years. This was destroyed during the Second World War.

**NAMES OF THE SYNAGOGUE**

Synagogue is not a Hebrew word (see p. 47), but comes from the Greek, and means a **meeting** or **assembly place**. The Hebrew word is **Beit Haknesset**, which means literally **house of assembly**. Since a synagogue has many functions, it is also known by various names:

**Beit Tefillah (House of Prayer),** because a synagogue is a place of

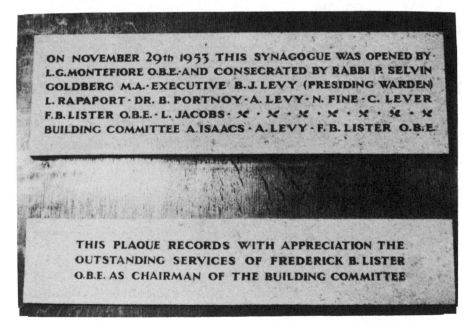

ON NOVEMBER 29th 1953 THIS SYNAGOGUE WAS OPENED BY L.G.MONTEFIORE O.B.E. AND CONSECRATED BY RABBI P. SELVIN GOLDBERG M.A. EXECUTIVE B.J. LEVY (PRESIDING WARDEN) L. RAPAPORT · DR. B. PORTNOY · A. LEVY · N. FINE · C. LEVER F.B. LISTER O.B.E. · L. JACOBS · ✗ · ✗ · ✗ · ✗ · ✗ · ✗ · ✗ BUILDING COMMITTEE A. ISAACS · A. LEVY · F.B. LISTER O.B.E.

THIS PLAQUE RECORDS WITH APPRECIATION THE OUTSTANDING SERVICES OF FREDERICK B. LISTER O.B.E. AS CHAIRMAN OF THE BUILDING COMMITTEE

A Polish synagogue

worship, and Jews regard praying with a congregation as very important.

**Beit Hamidrash (House of Study)**, because learning about prayer, worship and other aspects of the Jewish religion is just as important as praying and attending services.

**Beit Ha'Am (House of the People)**, because a synagogue is not made up of special people, such as priests or rabbis, but of ordinary Jews who conduct services and organise activities.

Many Jews refer to their synagogue as **shool**, which is a Yiddish word, similar to the German word for school. A few countries, such as America, tend to use the word **temple** instead of synagogue.

### TYPES OF SYNAGOGUES

The majority of Jews in Britain belong to **Orthodox** synagogues. Most Orthodox Jews originally come from Eastern and Central Europe, such as Poland and Russia, and are known as **Ashkenasim**. A smaller group of Orthodox Jews can trace their background to

Spain and North Africa. They are known as **Sefardim**. There are small differences between these groups, such as the way they read Hebrew and chant their prayer. Some Orthodox Jews are very strict and do not mix with other Jews or non-Jews.

There are other religious Jews who are not Orthodox. They call themselves **Reform, Liberal** or **Progressive**. Jackson's Row is a non-Orthodox synagogue, and uses the word **Reform** as part of its title. On p. 8 you will see a table which shows some of the differences between Orthodox and Reform synagogues.

**JEWISH AND CHRISTIAN WORSHIP**

Non-Jewish visitors to Jackson's Row may find that whilst there are many differences, in some ways the service is very similar to the service in a Christian church. Both have congregational prayers, recitation of psalms, and a sermon. Most non-Jews will not be familiar with the Hebrew prayers, nor understand them. But there is one word which is often used and which most people will know. It is **Amen**, which roughly translated means **so may it be**. It is a very ancient word and can be found in many parts of the Bible, such as Numbers 5: 22. Another well-known Hebrew word used in the synagogue but again known by many non-Jews is **Hallelujah**, meaning **praise the Lord!**

**SOME DIFFERENCES IN JEWISH WORSHIP**

|  | **Orthodox** | **Jackson's Row** |
|---|---|---|
| Sabbath Eve Service begins | 15 minutes before sunset, between 3.30 p.m. and 5.30 p.m. during winter months and usually no later than 9.00 p.m. during summer months. | 6.00 p.m. through-out the year. |
| Sabbath Morning Service begins | Around 9.00 a.m. | 11.00 a.m. |
| Length of Sabbath Morning Service | 2¼–3 hours. | 1¼–1½ hours. |

7

| Language used at services | Only Hebrew used, with exception of prayer for Royal Family and State of Israel. | About 60% Hebrew, 40% English. |
|---|---|---|
| Form of service | Prayers are chanted. Larger synagogues have male choirs. | Prayers are usually read. A choir of both men and women leads the singing. |
| Music | All singing is done without any musical instrument. | An organ is used. |
| Seating | Men and boys sit in the main part of the synagogue. Women and girls sit apart, usually in an upper room, known as the **Gallery**, sometimes on the same level, but behind the men, or sometimes in another room. Members have their own seats. | Men, women and children sit together. There are no reserved seats. |
| Officiants | Usually conducted by **Cantor (Reader)** or Rabbi or any other male. | Usually conducted by Rabbi or other male or female. |

# 3. Inside Jackson's Row Synagogue

Jackson's Row is one of the oldest and largest synagogues in Manchester. The original building was consecrated in 1858 and was given a Hebrew name which means **Holy Congregation – Gate of Zion**.

Nowadays some 450 families belong to Jackson's Row. Since many of these people worship there regularly, they need a large room in which to hold their services. This is the most important part of the synagogue. At Jackson's Row it is divided into two sections. The main part is on the ground floor and is used by most people. There is also a gallery. Although some members of the congregation like to sit here each week, it is mainly used when there is a special service and a large congregation is expected.

### THE ARK

The most important feature of any synagogue is the **Aron Hakodesh**, the **Holy Ark**. The Ark is the cabinet in which the Scrolls of the Torah are kept. It is like a very large cupboard and is placed on a platform against the wall at the front or east end of the synagogue. This is the direction of the Holy City of Jerusalem and worshippers always face that way.

It is the Ark that makes a synagogue and today it is regarded as taking the place of the Ark of the Covenant described in the Bible. You can read about it in Exodus 25. Jackson's Row has a most beautiful ark. There are a number of Jewish symbols found on its doors. They include the **shofar**, or **ram's horn**, the **Menorah** or **seven-branched candlestick** and the **mezuzah**, a small case which contains a piece of parchment on which Hebrew prayers are written. Jewish families also put a mezuzah on the doorposts of most rooms in their home. Although the Ark doors are rather heavy, they slide open easily, but before anything inside can be seen, the curtain must be drawn to the sides. Then a whole line of Torah scrolls is in full view, each scroll beautifully dressed in blue mantles and various silver objects, all of which we shall speak about presently.

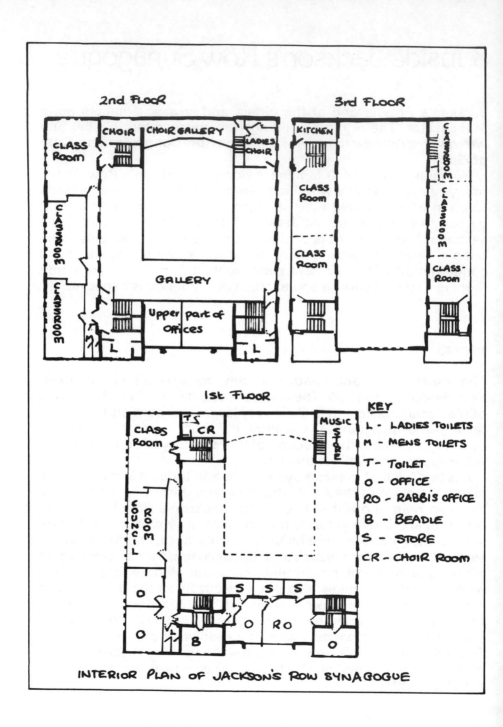

**2nd FLOOR**

CLASS ROOM
CHOIR
CHOIR GALLERY
LADIES CHOIR
CLASSROOM
CLASSROOM
GALLERY
Upper part of Offices
L
L

**3rd FLOOR**

KITCHEN
CLASSROOM
CLASS ROOM
CLASS ROOM
CLASSROOM
CLASS-ROOM

**1st FLOOR**

CLASS ROOM
T
CR
MUSIC STORE
CLASSROOM
O
S
S
S
O
B
O
RO
O

**KEY**

L - LADIES TOILETS
M - MENS TOILETS
T - TOILET
O - OFFICE
RO - RABBI'S OFFICE
B - BEADLE
S - STORE
CR - CHOIR ROOM

INTERIOR PLAN OF JACKSON'S ROW SYNAGOGUE

The Holy Ark and the Scrolls it contains.

## AROUND THE ARK

Immediately above the Ark there is a tablet with the Ten Commandments written in Hebrew. Above this there is another single line of Hebrew writing. Just as some schools have a motto, so synagogues have a verse from the Bible. Jackson's Row has words from Psalm 69: 13, 'As for me, may my prayer come before You, O Lord in an acceptable time.' Hanging before the Ark is a little lamp. In Hebrew the lamp is called **Ner Tamid** meaning the **Everlasting Light**. It is never switched off and is a reminder that this is God's House, and His presence remains here, even when there are no worshippers in the synagogue.

## THE TORAH SCROLLS

There are eight Torah Scrolls in the Ark but the number will vary from synagogue to synagogue. They all contain the same text, namely the first five books of the Bible, often called the **Five Books of Moses**. Ideally a synagogue should have three Scrolls, for there are three separate readings during the Day of Atonement service. However, over the years, families often donate a Scroll, sometimes in memory of a loved one who has died, and so synagogues have extra Scrolls. Some of the Torah Scrolls at Jackson's Row are around one hundred years old. Every few years they have to be checked, but after a while they can no longer be used. They must not be thrown away or in any way destroyed since they are still regarded as very precious as they contain God's holy words. Instead, they are buried in a Jewish cemetery. For centuries, Torah Scrolls have been handwritten. This practice continues today. All the Scrolls in the Ark have been written by an expert **scribe** called a **sofer**. When a synagogue needs a new Scroll it will ask a scribe to write one. A newly written Scroll in 1983 would cost about £6,000. The parchment alone costs around £1,000 to buy. Next, there is the time it takes to complete a Scroll. It will take a sofer, working full-time, one whole year to complete one Scroll.

## DRESSING THE SCROLL

Before a Scroll can be placed in the Ark, it needs to be **dressed**. This means it needs a **mantle**. The colour can vary, but at Jackson's Row it is blue. All synagogues, however, change to white during

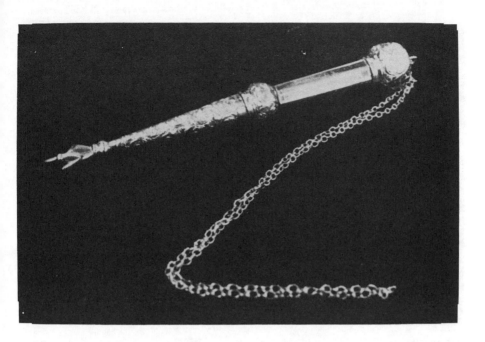

Jewish New Year and Day of Atonement services. Silver items are placed over the mantle. There is the **breastplate** which often contains the emblems of the Twelve Tribes of Israel. Over this comes the **yad** or **pointer** which will be used when reading from the Scroll. Finally there are the **bells** or **crown** which are placed over the wooden rollers. Both of these can be found on the various Scrolls at Jackson's Row.


## READING DESK

In front of the Ark is the **Reading** (or **Reader's**) **Desk**, which at Jackson's Row is also used as the **pulpit**. The Torah Scroll is also placed here and read. Both the Ark and Desk stand on a raised platform known as the **Bimah**. In most Orthodox synagogues, the Ark and the Reading Desk are separate. The Reading Desk is usually in the centre of the synagogue, where the officiant faces the Ark. At Jackson's Row, and most other Progressive synagogues, the person leading the service faces the congregation with his back to the Ark for most of the service.

**THE CHOIR**

There has been a choir at Jackson's Row since the very early days of the congregation. It is made up of a number of men and women who lead other congregants in the sung parts of the services. Some fifty years ago the choir was in great demand and was invited to sing at some Orthodox synagogues in Manchester, especially at weddings, civic services and memorial services. To this day it is one of the finest synagogue choirs in the country. At Jackson's Row the choir is in full view of the congregation but many other synagogue choirs are hidden from view.

**JEWISH SYMBOLS**

All synagogues should have windows. At Jackson's Row they help to beautify the synagogue since they are made of stained-glass. They are very colourful and show scenes from the Bible.

Two Jewish symbols can be seen around the synagogue. The best known is perhaps the **Magen David**, the **Shield** (or **Star**) **of David**. It consists of a triangle with another one placed over it

upside down. They make a six-pointed star. Although named after the biblical King David, its use as a Jewish symbol is not ancient. It has also been used by non-Jews, especially in churches.

The other, older, Jewish symbol is the **Menorah** and is mentioned in the Bible, for example in Exodus 25: 31–37. The biblical Menorah was a seven-branched candlestick, but the one used in synagogues and Jewish homes during the winter festival of Chanukah has nine branches and is sometimes called a **Chanukiyah**. The seven-branched Menorah is the official emblem of the State of Israel, whilst the Magen David is found on the flag of Israel. Both emblems are combined at Jackson's Row in one of the lights around the Bimah.

At the side of the Bimah, there is a door leading to the **Room of Prayer**. This is used for short services such as a weekday evening service. At the back of the synagogue, there are bookcases which contain copies of the prayer book. They are mainly intended for the use of visitors, since Jackson's Row congregants are encouraged to buy their own copies.

## THE FOYER

The foyer is rather large and people often chat there before the start of the service. They may look at the notice boards or read some of the magazines and other literature on display. There are also Bibles that can be used to follow the Torah readings. It is also possible for a Jewish male visitor to borrow a **tallit**, a **prayer-shawl**. A non-Jewish male visitor may borrow a **yamulkah**, a **skullcap**. It is an old Jewish custom for men and boys to cover their heads during prayers. It was considered a sign of respect. Near the main entrance of the synagogue there is the **Bride's Room** reserved for the bride and her near female relatives prior to her wedding ceremony.

So far we have described the most important part of any synagogue building, the **sanctuary**, as some call it. At Jackson's Row there is also a floor above and below. Downstairs there are the hall and a number of other rooms, many of which can be joined onto the hall, thus making it much larger. Since many social and educational events take place at Jackson's Row, they need a large hall. The well-equipped kitchens are also found on this level, as well as a number of toilets. The upper floors include the general office,

A prayer shawl and skull caps.

rabbi's study, and the office of the General Secretary. The rabbi's study contains a library. The windows in his study have two of the emblems already mentioned, namely the Magen David and the Menorah. This floor also contains a number of toilets. There are many parts to Jackson's Row, but it is the people and their activities which make it a living community. In the next chapters we shall see how the synagogue is used religiously, educationally and socially.

# 4. The Rabbi and his work

A rabbi in some ways is like a clergyman of the Christian religion. This is because he conducts services, officiates at various ceremonies, and visits the sick. However, a rabbi is firstly a teacher of the Jewish religion (**rabbi** in Hebrew means **teacher**), and it is his task to bring to his people God's message and laws. By his teaching and preaching, he will help them to understand and love their Jewish heritage. He is the spiritual leader of the synagogue and is there to give guidance, encouragement and comfort whenever the need arises. The rabbi is a friend to young and old alike. Progressive Judaism allows women to train as rabbis but this is forbidden within Orthodox Judaism. At present, the Progressive movement in Britain has ordained four women. They serve as rabbis of London synagogues. One of them in fact was brought up at Jackson's Row. Some synagogue ministers are not rabbis but have the title **Reverend**. This means that they lack a deeper knowledge in rabbinic studies. However, they usually carry out all the duties of a rabbi.

Jackson's Row synagogue is fortunate to have a young and energetic rabbi. He trained at a Jewish theological college in London for five years before being **ordained** and given the title of rabbi.

It is usual for a rabbi to be married. The rabbi of Jackson's Row is supported in his work by his wife and children. His wife is a member of the synagogue choir and she also works full time.

## A BUSY LIFE

Since Jackson's Row is a large and thriving synagogue, its rabbi leads a very busy life. Most weekdays he can be found in his study at the synagogue. Many of his congregants will come to see him to arrange a wedding or a funeral, or perhaps to discuss a personal problem. Others may find a telephone call the most useful way of making contact.

There will be days when the rabbi is out and about. He may be at a meeting of rabbis in London or in another northern city, or have a number of house and hospital visits to make. He may be a guest speaker at a luncheon or conducting a happy ceremony such as a wedding or a sad ceremony such as a funeral.

The rabbi's day does not finish around five in the afternoon. Most evenings will be taken up with meetings with groups such as the synagogue council, the wardens or the synagogue education committee or perhaps he will visit the youth club. Weekends too are busy periods. In addition to regular Sabbath services, Sunday is a popular day for Jewish weddings. Sometimes two or three can take place in one afternoon! Rabbis usually take off one day in the week. At Jackson's Row the rabbi makes Wednesday his free day.

## HOLDING OFFICE

The rabbi at Jackson's Row also finds time to work with many organisations in Manchester and elsewhere. These include the **Assembly of Rabbis of the Reform Synagogues**, which is a national organisation. Other organisations are Manchester-based such as the **Council of Christians and Jews**, the **Council of Faiths**, and the **Anglo-Israel Friendship League**.

All male Jews wear the tallit and cover their heads when they go to the Synagogue.

## SPECIAL CLOTHES

When he is conducting a service the rabbi wears special clothes. These consist of a black gown and hat. On the Day of Atonement and at New Year, the gown and hat are white. In some synagogues, the rabbi simply wears his ordinary clothes and, like any other male Jew, has a tallit over his shoulders and a yamulkah on his head.

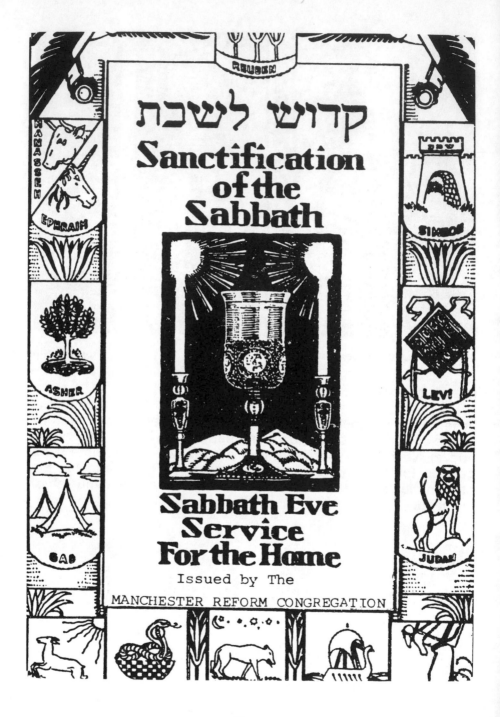

קדוש לשבת

# Sanctification of the Sabbath

## Sabbath Eve Service For the Home

Issued by The

MANCHESTER REFORM CONGREGATION

# 5. Services of worship

In many ways Jackson's Row is a community centre since it puts on so many different activities and appeals to all age groups. Its main task, however, is to be a worshipping community, and so its spiritual life is built around its religious services. Its major weekly service takes place on Saturday, the Jewish Sabbath. This is a special day for the Jews. They remember that God rested on the seventh day after he had created the world and all that is in it (see Genesis 2: 2, 3). One of the Ten Commandments tells Jews that they too must rest on the Sabbath (see Exodus 20: 8–11).

The service begins at 11.00 a.m. and lasts for about one and a half hours. The Sabbath eve service begins at 6.00 p.m. on Friday and lasts for not much more than forty minutes. Most Progressive synagogues have a later service beginning around 8.00 p.m. and lasting for an hour. Since Jackson's Row is in the heart of the city of Manchester, an earlier service, straight after work, is more appealing for those already in the city centre. Orthodox synagogues have their Sabbath eve services at different times according to the season of the year. For example, in the summer, services start at 8.00 p.m. whilst in winter as early as 3.30 p.m. Their morning services usually begin around 9.00 a.m. and last about two and a half hours.

**SABBATH IN THE HOME**

Friday night is a very happy and relaxing time for Jackson's Row families. The week has ended, **Shabbat**, the Sabbath, has begun. People enjoy an unhurried meal, free from watching television or rushing out to the cinema or a disco. These things can be done on other nights. Friday night in Jewish homes is special. The family is together and welcomes in the **Queen Sabbath**. The mother lights the candles and says the blessing. The father recites the **Kiddush**, the blessings over the wine, and all present drink the wine. The blessing is said over the **challot**, the special twisted loaves of bread. Wife and children are also blessed and all greet each other with the words, **Shabbat shalom, a peaceful Sabbath**. During the meal, the family will sing Sabbath songs. Some will be very old whilst others will be from Israel and new. After the meal the entire

family will recite the **grace after meals**. Although it is rather long, it is welcomed by all due to its joyful melodies. It is a perfect and restful start to the Sabbath.

### SABBATH MORNING WORSHIP

Congregants look forward to coming to Jackson's Row on Saturday morning. It is a chance for friends to meet and chat. Before the service there is quite a buzz of conversation but at 11.00 there is a hushed silence as the service begins. The main part of the Sabbath morning service is the reading from the Torah. The Ark is opened, a Torah Scroll is taken out and held by a warden or other member. After some prayers it is carried around the synagogue. Some congregants bow before it as a sign that it is God's holy word.

### THE TORAH READING

Each Sabbath a portion of the Torah is chanted or read. It takes a year to complete the reading of the whole Scroll. At Jackson's

Orthodox Jews.

Row, the reading is about thirty verses long. This is the pattern in Progressive synagogues. In Orthodox synagogues, the reading is much longer. At Jackson's Row, at least three people are **called up** to the reading when they recite various blessings. Many Progressive synagogues only call up one person, whereas Orthodox synagogues usually call up seven, all of whom have to be males over the age of thirteen. After the reading, there is an **elevation**. A person lifts and opens the Torah Scroll so that all the congregation can see its text. It is then dressed by another person, often assisted by young children. At Jackson's Row as well as some other Progressive synagogues, they elevate the Scroll before the reading as well as after.

**THE READING FROM THE PROPHETS**

In addition to the Torah reading there is the **haftara**, the reading from the prophets. At Jackson's Row and other Progressive synagogues, it is usually read in English, but sometimes Bar Mitzvah boys will read it in Hebrew (see p. 39). In Orthodox synagogues, it is chanted in Hebrew, although the chant is a little different from the one used for the Torah reading.

## SPECIAL PRAYERS

After the readings from the Scripture, a number of special prayers are recited. They include prayers for the recovery of ill members, for the welfare of the congregation and for the Queen, the Royal Family and the State of Israel. The latter prayers, like other important ones, are recited when the congregation is standing. Otherwise Jewish prayers are said when the congregation is sitting. After these prayers, the Torah is again carried around the synagogue, and as before, many worshippers bow before it, or some even take the fringes of their tallit to the Torah, and then kiss the tallit. This is another form of respect for the Torah. After the Torah Scroll has been returned to the Ark, the rabbi will then give his sermon. He may take as his theme a topic from one of the Scriptural readings. He may, instead, speak about an event that has happened during the week. Often he will include stories from the rabbinic literature. When the rabbi is away, the executive of Jackson's Row invite a Guest Preacher.

## CHILDREN'S SERVICE

Young children may find an adult service a little difficult to understand. At Jackson's Row, there are children's services on the first Saturday in the month. Some synagogues have them every week. Although an adult is present, the service is conducted by the children themselves and is very much enjoyed by all those who attend. Some of these children are not members of Jackson's Row, but they are still very welcome.

## GETTING TOGETHER

After the service, the whole congregation is invited to Kiddush held in the lower hall. This Hebrew word means **holy**. Everyone present joins in singing some biblical verses dealing with the importance of keeping the Sabbath. Then a blessing is sung over wine and everyone drinks from their glass. Young children are usually given orange juice. The two loaves of challot are blessed and broken up. A piece is given to every person. Sometimes any important messages about forthcoming activities or special services are given out. This is a good opportunity for people to chat to one another and to welcome any visitors who may be

present. These may include members of other synagogues. Non-Jews also come. They are interested in learning about Jewish worship. Since Jackson's Row congregants are very friendly all these visitors are made to feel at home and are invited to ask questions about Jewish worship in general and worship at Jackson's Row in particular.

### AUTUMN FESTIVALS

The two most important Jewish festivals are **Rosh Hashanah (New Year)** and **Yom Kippur (the Day of Atonement)**. They are known as **High Holydays**.

Most Jews go to the synagogue on these days so Jackson's Row can expect its largest congregations of the year. In the past there was not enough room for all the members to meet together so the congregation had to hire a large hall nearby.

### NEW YEAR

Rosh Hashanah, the Jewish New Year, is celebrated in September or early October (the Jewish month of **Tishri**). This is not really as

strange as it might seem. Many ancient peoples such as the Persians and Greeks began their year in autumn. In fact, 1st January was not accepted as New Year's Day in England until the 18th century.

At Rosh Hashanah, Jews send greetings to their relatives and friends. There are special cards with pictures of Israel or New Year symbols. Many are produced by Jewish charities. Some members in Manchester prefer to put a message in one of the Jewish newspapers such as the national *Jewish Chronicle* or the local *Jewish Gazette* or *Jewish Telegraph*. Synagogues such as Jackson's Row also send their members a card with details of the special New Year services to be held. Most Jews keep two days for Rosh Hashanah. There will be services on both of them but the first day is more important. Then the service will last all morning.

The festival really starts the evening before the service, with a ceremony at home. In addition to Kiddush, all the family will dip a piece of apple into honey and eat it. Then everyone joins in a special blessing: 'May it be your will, Lord, our Lord, and God of our fathers, that the coming year will be a happy and sweet one!'

Blowing the shofar.

## BLOWING THE HORN

The highlight of the Rosh Hashanah morning service is without doubt the blowing of the **shofar**. Although the synagogue is full, you can hear a pin drop before the stirring notes of the shofar break the silence. It is a wonderful moment for all present as they listen to the unique sound of one of the oldest instruments in the world. In all, they will hear one hundred notes. These remind every worshipper that the festival is a day of judgement and that God is King. He will forgive people their sins if they sincerely ask him to do so.

## THE DAY OF ATONEMENT

The New Year celebration lasts for ten days, ending with Yom Kippur, the Day of Atonement. Jackson's Row members, together with fellow Jews all over the world, will fast on that day. No food can be eaten for at least twenty-five hours and in addition, no drink, not even a glass of water, will pass the lips of Jews. There are some people who cannot, and indeed, must not fast. This includes children under Bar or Bat Mitzvah age, although some older children are encouraged to fast for part of the day, or at least to give up eating sweets and crisps! Pregnant women and ill or elderly people who need to take medicine or pills every day also do not fast.

There will be a very large congregation at Jackson's Row on Yom Kippur. Prayers will be recited from 11.00 a.m. until around 7.00 p.m. Most Orthodox synagogues will begin even earlier, around 8.00 a.m. Many prayers will be repeated a number of times, and the rabbi will give more than one sermon. The morning service will be the best attended, since the whole family will be at worship together. Mothers with young children tend to return home in order to prepare a meal for the children, whilst father remains in the synagogue. Some people find that fasting gives them a headache, and they need fresh air. The synagogue will again be crowded in the later afternoon for the **Yizkor** service, which especially attracts the older members. Then many worshippers remember their dead relatives and say special prayers. It is a very moving occasion and is followed by **Neilah**, the closing or concluding service. The Ark will be opened many times during this service. Some synagogues even keep the Ark opened all the time.

Everyone looks forward to hearing the shofar at this time. Unlike Rosh Hashanah, when one hundred notes are sounded, there will be just one long sound, a stirring end to a long day. It is as if God is saying, 'I have forgiven your sins.'

The High Holyday period may seem rather gloomy and sad, but when you enter the synagogue you will find the Ark, curtain, the Torah scroll covers, even the rabbi's gown, decked in white, the colour of purity. White flowers are placed on the Bimah, so the whole sanctuary looks bright and different.

### HARVEST FESTIVAL

A few days after Yom Kippur sees a much happier mood amongst Jackson's Row members. Another festival is being celebrated; this time it is **Succot**, also known as **Tabernacles** or **Booths**. A booth **(succah)** is a type of hut and is erected a day or so before the festival by synagogue members. They decorate it with masses of foliage and hang posters or children's paintings on the walls. Fruit is also used. This will be taken to local hospitals and old age homes when the festival has finished a week later.

Inside a Succah.

Orthodox synagogues have their succah outside at the back, whereas at Jackson's Row, it is made in an inside room with a glass roof, so that the sky can be seen. There can be problems with an outside succah especially if it rains. Some individual families will build a succah in their own homes. Many will invite friends to visit it and to have a meal in it. Some people will even take their beds into it and sleep there for a week.

During the festival, a special ceremony takes place. At the morning services, certain 'plants' are waved. These are known as the **Four Species** and are named in Leviticus 23: 40. There is the **palm branch** which has tied to it leaves from the **myrtle** and **willow**. The fourth item is described in the Bible as 'fruit from a goodly tree'. This is taken to be the **etrog**, a beautifully smelling, yellow fruit like a very large lemon. It does not grow in Britain so the congregation at Jackson's Row have to import it from Israel or California or some other very hot country. It will cost at least £20.

### DANCING IN THE SYNAGOGUE

The last day of the festival is regarded by many as a new and separate festival. It is known as **Simchat Torah**, the rejoicing over the Torah. It is one of the few occasions in the year when every Torah Scroll is removed from the Ark and carried in procession right around the synagogue. This is followed by the children who carry flags, often made by themselves. After each procession, which is called a **Hakafah** or **circuit**, those who carry the scrolls dance with them in front of the Ark, with the children joining in. The rest of the congregation clap hands and sing. The atmosphere during this service is rather different from other services held at Jackson's Row. In many Orthodox synagogues, the women throw sweets from the gallery to the children below. It is a fitting end to a month of festivals and is thoroughly enjoyed by adults and children alike.

### CHANUKAH

Around the time when Christians are celebrating Christmas, the Jewish community will be enjoying one of its own festivals known as **Chanukah**. This eight-day festival is also known as the **Festival of Lights** and it reminds Jews of a story about one of their great heroes, **Judah Maccabee (Judas Maccabeus)** and his miraculous

jar of oil. Judah lived 2,000 years ago when the Greeks ruled over Israel. They did not worship God and tried to stop the Jews doing so. They set up statues of their own gods in the Temple at Jerusalem. When Judah and his men conquered the Greeks, they knew that they must make the Temple pure again and fit for worship. They threw out the Greek statues and set up the lamp which had to burn always in the Temple. But when they came to light the lamp, they discovered that there was only one jar of the special oil which had to be used and it would last for only one night. It took eight days to obtain more of the pure oil and in all that time, the story says, the lamp burned. One jar of oil had kept it alight. Judah decreed that Jews should remember this special occasion and so the Festival of Lights came into being.

Although Chanukah is regarded as a minor festival which means that people do not have to take time off work or school to go to the synagogue, it is one of the most popular celebrations at Jackson's Row. Each of the eight nights of Chanukah, the family will gather together at home round the nine-branched candlestick known as the **Chanukiyah** or Menorah. They will say blessings and sing songs about the festival as they light a candle known as the servant. From its flame they light the other candles, on the first night one other, on the second two and so on so that at the end of the festival all nine candles of the Chanukiyah shine out.

The children will be given presents during the festival. Some lucky children get presents every day of the festival. They will also play with a special spinning top known as a **sevivon** or **dreidle**. Special foods will be eaten including the popular **latkes**, a sort of potato cake.

During the festival, some of the children will put on a play or musical at the synagogue. They often write their own scripts and make their own costumes. These pantomimes are usually given seasonal names such as *The Magic Menorah* or *Alice in Chanukahland*.

### PURIM

Another minor festival is **Purim**. It takes place around March and is a joyful occasion. At Purim the Jews remember how Queen Esther saved her countrymen when they were in exile in Persia. There the wicked chief minister, Haman, plotted to destroy the Jews but Esther risked her life to tell the king about the plans. You can read

the full story in the book of Esther in the Bible.

The children at Jackson's Row particularly look forward to the reading of the scroll. Every time the villain, Haman, is mentioned, the children make as much noise as possible, with the approval of their parents and other adults. They come to the synagogue 'armed' for the occasion. They bring drums, whistles, football rattles, even saucepan lids, and the whole synagogue echoes with the sound.

As with Chanukah, children put on plays at the synagogue, this time with a Purim theme, and it is also the custom to have fancy dress competitions. Everyone will also enjoy the tea which will include the special Purim cakes called **hamantaschen**, named after the three-cornered hat which Haman wore.

### FESTIVAL OF SPRING AND FREEDOM

A month later Jewish families celebrate **Pesach (Passover)**. This is probably the best known and loved of all the festivals. At this time, the Jews remember how God helped them escape from the land of Egypt over 3,000 years ago. You can read about this in Exodus 12 in the Bible. The Festival lasts for a week and mainly takes place in the home although there will be special services at Jackson's Row. The days before the festival are busy for the Jewish housewife. She will do a lot of extra baking and cleaning. Passover brings a number of restrictions with it, such as not eating bread or food with yeast in it. Only **matzot (unleavened bread)** is allowed in Jewish homes during the festival. This is because when the Jews escaped from Egypt they did not have time to let their bread rise, so had to bake it without yeast or leaven. Some families will search through the house and any ordinary bread or crumbs found will be burned.

The festival begins with a celebration on the first evening, known as **seder**, a Hebrew word meaning **order**. A dish or plate is placed on the dining table. It contains some special and unusual items, such as a roasted egg, bitter herbs and a mixture called **charoset**, made up of chopped apple sprinkled with a little wine and cinnamon. Some families add to this paste a few chopped nuts. These foods remind the families of the difficult time the Jews had in Egypt.

A traditional Passover dish.

At Passover, the people use a special book known as the **haggadah** which contains stories, prayers, and songs about the escape from Egypt. Some children have their own haggadah, with colourful pictures and Hebrew and English text.

At one point during the meal the youngest child stands up and asks, 'Why is this night different from all other nights?' The father of the family then usually tells the story of the last night that the Jews spent in Egypt and how they escaped with God's help. All the family share the unleavened bread and have four separate drinks of wine during the meal. There is much singing and by the end of this long meal the smaller children have usually nodded off.

Many families repeat the seder the following night, or will be invited to relatives or friends to join their celebrations. At Jackson's Row Synagogue there is a communal seder for 120 people, who perhaps have no family in the area. It is a strong Jewish tradition to make sure that no one is alone for the seder. It is important that everyone can celebrate the festival in a family or community. The rabbi will conduct the seder and everyone joins in, especially with the singing.

## THE LIFE OF A JEW

In addition to the festivals, there are other times in the year when members of Jackson's Row celebrate a happy event.

## BABY BLESSINGS

The ceremony of blessing a new born baby was introduced to the synagogue by the early leaders of Progressive Judaism. At Jackson's Row, it takes place during the Sabbath morning service. The parents bring their child before the Ark and, in front of the whole congregation, the rabbi gives the boy or girl both a Hebrew and an English name, followed by a special blessing. After the service, the parents invite the congregation to join with them in Kiddush and help their family **simcha** (joyful occasion).

## BAR MITZVAH

On certain Sabbaths, a special event takes place at Jackson's Row during the morning service. A boy will celebrate his **Bar Mitzvah** or a girl her **Bat Mitzvah**. Bar/Bat Mitzvah means **son/daughter of the commandment** or **Torah**. From that day the young person is regarded as a full member of the synagogue community and as responsible as any Jewish adult. A Bar Mitzvah usually takes place when a boy is thirteen years old. In an Orthodox synagogue a girl becomes Bat Mitzvah when she is twelve, but at Jackson's Row she waits until she is thirteen.

The main feature of the Bar Mitzvah ceremony in any synagogue is for the boy to chant or read passages from the Torah. Orthodox communities do not permit girls to read from the Torah and their ceremony, usually held on a Sunday afternoon, will involve them in reading passages from a printed Bible and prayer book. At Jackson's Row, the Bat Mitzvah ceremony is identical to the Bar Mitzvah. Each Bar/Bat Mitzvah is presented with a prayer book or Bible and certificates. It is a very proud day for both the young person and the parents, and often they will celebrate at a special lunch after the service in the synagogue hall. Sometimes instead, a dinner will be arranged the following evening when the Bar/Bat Mitzvah will give a little speech to thank parents for their love and help. It is a family occasion and relatives will come often from as far afield as America or Israel.

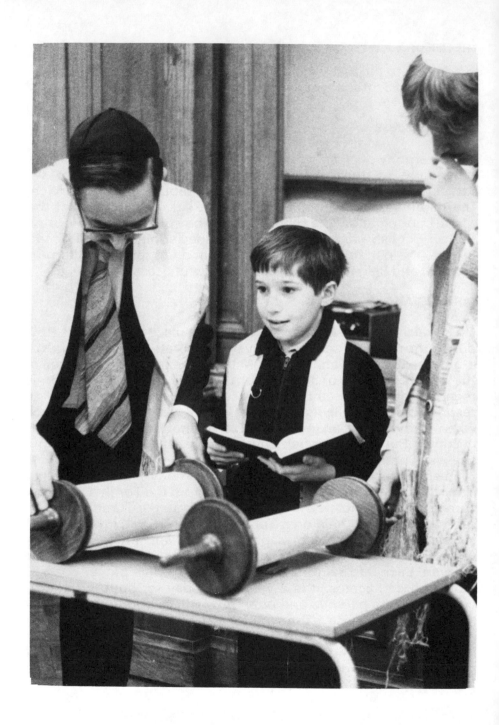

## WEDDINGS

About a dozen marriages are performed at Jackson's Row each year. Most Jewish weddings in Britain take place on a Sunday, usually early in the afternoon. Sabbath and festivals are considered joyful days and weddings do not take place then. It is better to spread the joy, rather than have two joyful events on the same day. There are also other days and periods when weddings cannot take place, especially in Orthodox synagogues, because of sad events in Jewish history.

For the wedding ceremony, a **chuppah** or **canopy** is put up in the synagogue near the Ark. It consists of a large piece of velvet cloth supported by four poles, one at each corner. The bride, bridegroom, parents, and often grandparents, will all stand under it, together with the rabbi. The bride and groom will drink wine from the same cup to show that in their future life together they will share all things. The groom will place a wedding ring on the bride's forefinger on the right hand and will recite a verse in Hebrew which says that she is now his wife according to the laws of the Jewish religion. The bride is then free to move the ring to the usual finger. At a Jackson's Row wedding, the bride will also make

On the    the    day
of the month of    in the year 57
corresponding to the
here in
The bridegroom        said to the
bride
Be my wife according to the Law of Moses and Israel & I will
cherish respect & support you in the faithful manner in which
sons in Israel cherish respect and support their wives.
And the bride        said to the
bridegroom
Be my husband according to the Law of Moses & Israel & I will
cherish respect & support you in the faithful manner in which
daughters in Israel cherish respect & support their husbands.
And the bride        agreed to
the proposal of the bridegroom.
And the bridegroom        agreed to
the proposal of the bride.
Accordingly they both entered into this covenant of love
and companionship of peace and friendship to create
a Jewish home to the glory of the Holy One blessed be
He who makes His people Israel holy through the holy
covenant of marriage.
This has taken place in our presence & is all valid & binding

a similar declaration, sometimes giving her future husband a ring. The rabbi will give a short talk to the newly married couple, and then read to them their **ketubah**, the **marriage certificate**, an important document. He will ask God to bless the couple in the years ahead.

The final act may seem rather strange to a first-time visitor. A small glass is placed on the floor, just in front of the groom, who raises his foot and stamps on the glass. No one knows for certain why this is done. Some say it is to remind those present that the Temple is in ruins and we mourn this and other sad events in Jewish history. Others say that marriage will not solve all problems, and there will be times when there is a little strain in a marriage which may bring some unhappiness. Life itself, like a glass, cannot last forever, and we should always remember this.

## FUNERALS

When a member of Jackson's Row dies, the relatives can leave all the details of the funeral arrangements to the synagogue secretary. The burial will take place as soon as possible, usually the following day, unless it is a Sabbath or festival. Orthodox Judaism forbids cremation but Jackson's Row does allow it. The synagogue's present cemetery is part of the City Council's cemetery. After the funeral, special daily prayers will be said in the home of the near relatives, taken by the rabbi, or by a member of the synagogue, who perhaps was a friend of the dead person. Some families have these home services for a week, others just for one to three days. It is good to know that a person or family suffering the loss of a loved one can get much comfort from members of the synagogue.

# 6. How the Synagogue is organised

Jackson's Row Synagogue is run by some very active and dedicated members for the benefit of all the congregation. They are elected by the membership who are present at the **Annual General Meeting**, which takes place in April. The meeting is chaired by the **President**. He also heads the **Executive** which is made up of seven people. Many synagogues elect an honorary secretary, but since Jackson's Row is a large congregation, it enjoys the services of a full time official, known as the General Secretary. He is responsible to the Executive and is in charge of the day to day running of the synagogue. He is assisted by a secretary-typist. In addition to the Executive, a further ten men and women serve on the **Council**. Members who have served the synagogue for many years are often made life members of the Council. There are usually five such members. Although the rabbi is not an elected member, he attends both Executive and Council meetings. Executive members serve for just one year in their particular position.

There are also many committees which direct education, organise social functions or deal with repairs or the painting of parts of the building. All these committees meet at least three times a year.

## BECOMING A MEMBER

Jews join a synagogue by paying a subscription. The amount varies from synagogue to synagogue and from town to town. The present fee for family membership at Jackson's Row is £160 per year. This may seem rather a high figure, but there is no collection during services, and the fee also includes tuition for education, and burial costs. No synagogue will ever refuse membership to a person or family who cannot afford the subscription, and many members pay well below the official fee. Richer members are asked to give more, whilst all members are invited to make donations to charities, a very important act in the Jewish religion. Jackson's Row has an annual appeal, and the money collected is divided amongst a number of charities, local institutions or national charities, both Jewish and non-Jewish. A sizeable amount is always collected for charitable and educational organisations in Israel. Synagogue services and functions are open to both members and non-members alike, but only members can stand for office or vote at the A.G.M.

## BELONGING TO OTHER ORGANISATIONS

Although Jackson's Row proudly runs its own affairs as directed by its members, it also works closely with other organisations, both local and national. It is represented on the **Jewish Representative Council of Greater Manchester and Region**. The Council includes all Jewish organisations, not just synagogues. Jackson's Row also appoints two delegates to the **Board of Deputies of British Jews**, the most important Jewish organisation in Britain. Often its leaders speak to Government and other official agencies on behalf of the entire Jewish community. The Board of Deputies was founded in 1760 and whilst its headquarters are in London, a few of its meetings take place in Manchester and other provincial cities.

Jackson's Row is a founder member of the **Reform Synagogues of Great Britain**, an organisation to which some thirty Reform congregations belong. It nominates three members to serve on the R.S.G.B. Council and to attend its annual conference in June. In turn, the R.S.G.B. is part of the **World Union for Progressive Judaism**, an international body of Reform and Liberal synagogues. It was founded in London in 1926 but now has its headquarters in Jerusalem. There are member synagogues in some twenty-five countries, including Curaçao, Guatemala and Zimbabwe.

# 7. The Synagogue School

As we have seen, a synagogue is more than just a place of worship. Nearly every synagogue has special classes for children. They may be called the **cheder**, a Hebrew word for **room**, or just **Hebrew and Religion Classes**. At Jackson's Row they are known as **Religion School**. Whatever the name, the aims are the same: to enable Jewish children to learn about their religion and heritage. In many ways it is similar to the Christian Sunday school.

The Religion School at Jackson's Row meets on Sunday mornings, with some children also coming one evening during the week. At present there are about sixty members, between the ages of three and fifteen, although most tend to leave after their Bar or Bat Mitzvah at thirteen. A number of the children from Jackson's Row also go to Jewish day schools such as the King David School in Manchester.

**SUBJECTS LEARNED**

The religion school has about forty sessions each year. They cover the following subjects:

**Hebrew**: Jewish children will be introduced to Hebrew from a very early age. Since they learn Hebrew for only forty minutes a week, it is unlikely that they will be able to speak it, apart from a few simple sentences. The main purpose for teaching Hebrew is that youngsters will be able to follow, and later take part in a service. The children will also learn Hebrew songs, both those used at synagogue services and those folk songs sung in modern Israel.

**Religious Knowledge**: The Jewish religion has many ceremonies, customs and festivals. These all have to be covered in this session. There will, however, be lessons on the Sabbath and festivals, the **kosher** food laws, prayer and specific ceremonies. Kosher food is an important part of the Jewish religion. It means that Jewish people do not eat certain animals such as the pig, rabbit and shell-fish. They also buy their meat from a kosher butcher. You can find the full list of those animals that can and cannot be eaten, in Leviticus 11.

**History:** The Jews are an ancient people with a long history. A junior class will learn about biblical heroes such as Abraham, Moses, David and Elijah, whilst older children will hear about some of the early rabbis such as Hillel and Akiba.

Many new and exciting books are used at the Jackson's Row Religion School. Children will also see filmstrips and slides and hear records and cassettes, so learning about their religion can be fun. At the end of the summer term in July, each child is given a report and there is also the prizegiving ceremony. The teachers are part-time, and some give of their time without any payment. A number teach in schools during the week, whilst others do other jobs but have a knowledge they wish to share with the young people. Another group which has a concern for the Religion School is the **Parent-Teacher Association** which arranges parties, outings, and other activities throughout the year.

The Religion School is one of the most important groups of the entire synagogue, since it is the youngsters of today who will be

the leaders of Jackson's Row Synagogue in future years.

A recent development at Jackson's Row is the setting up of the **Northern Resources Centre**. This is a large room containing hundreds of books, slides, records and posters which can be used in the classroom. It serves not only the Religion School at Jackson's Row, but also the Religion Schools of other Reform synagogues in Manchester, Leeds, Southport and Blackpool. Teachers come from all these places to see what is available.

# 8.The Synagogue in the community

You do not have to be a member of Jackson's Row in order to join in the many activities arranged by the various committees. A long time ago, a famous Jewish teacher urged the people not to separate themselves from the community and this advice is still followed by both the leaders and members of Jackson's Row.


## THE LADIES' GUILD

No synagogue can run well without its **Ladies' Guild**, and certainly Jackson's Row is no exception. The Guild has regular meetings and its members play an essential role in all the affairs of the synagogue. Sometimes they discuss future activities arranged jointly by the Guild and other synagogue committees. There are times when the ladies work out a plan which will raise some money either for their own funds or for the synagogue or they arrange a rota for preparing the weekly Kiddush. They all prepare for jumble sales or coffee mornings or plan joint meetings with another Guild. They make sure too that beautiful flowers are on display in the sanctuary before a festival or special occasion.


## OTHER REGULAR ACTIVITIES

Since Jackson's Row has a large membership, it needs to put on a wide variety of activities which will satisfy all age groups and tastes. The following would be a typical diary of events for one week.

**Sunday:**
10.00 a.m.   Religion School
3.00 p.m.   Kung fu for martial arts enthusiasts
6.00 p.m.   Youth Group (13–16)

**Monday:**
7.30 p.m.   Outreach (a group of mentally handicapped adults)

**Tuesday:**
10.30 a.m.   Speakers' Class (to help those interested in public speaking)
 7.30 p.m.   University of Manchester Extra Mural Class

**Wednesday:**
 1.30 p.m.   Friendship Club (for Senior Citizens)
 6.00 p.m.   Beginner's Hebrew (for adults wishing to learn)

**Thursday:**
 7.30 p.m.   Ladies' Guild (monthly) or Council Meeting (monthly)

**Friday:**
 6.00 p.m.   Sabbath Eve Service

**Saturday:**
11.00 a.m.   Sabbath Morning Service
 7.30 p.m.   Youth Group (16 plus)

Other activities take place from time to time. They may take the form of a luncheon, a youth weekend, or a day's outing for the children of the Religion School. On many occasions, the synagogue's **Judaica Shop** will be open. It sells a wide range of religious items, so that people can purchase books or ritual objects for themselves, their children, or for presents. Many of the activities at Jackson's Row attract a large number of people who are not members of the synagogue. Some of the meetings are advertised in the local Jewish newspapers, but a full diary of events is printed in the weekly newsheet, or in Jackson's Row magazine, *The Grapevine*, which is published about three times a year.

## INTER-FAITH ACTIVITIES

Ever since Jackson's Row was founded, its members have made every effort to be on friendly terms with their Christian neighbours. Over the years, countless groups from churches and schools have visited Jackson's Row to learn a little about the Jewish religion. One outstanding event took place in January 1967. The late Cardinal John Heenan, who was then the leader of the Roman Catholic Church in England and Wales, visited Jackson's Row Synagogue for a Sabbath morning service and addressed the congregation. It was a very happy occasion and was reported in the Jewish and Catholic weekly newspapers.

In more recent times, Manchester has attracted people of faiths other than Christianity and Judaism. Members of Jackson's Row have also been involved in making contacts with members of these other religions so that true harmony can exist amongst people of all religions.

## OUTSIDE THE SYNAGOGUE

It is not only in the religious area where Jackson's Row members involve themselves. Some are very active in local politics, and many have served on the local council. One member was even a former Labour cabinet minister, and another was Lord Mayor. Other members play active roles in various other organisations, both Jewish and non-Jewish and they are proud of their involvement in so many areas of life in the city.

# 9. Over to you

It is hoped that you have enjoyed your brief visit to the Manchester Reform Synagogue. Perhaps your next step will be a real visit to a local synagogue. There are many synagogues in Britain, from Aberdeen to Southampton, and chances are that there will be one fairly near where you live. If you do not know of a local synagogue you may find that your reference library has a copy of the **Jewish Year Book** which lists all synagogues, and other organisations, with their addresses, or you can always write to:

> The Central Jewish Lecture and Information Committee
> Board of Deputies
> Woburn House, Upper Woburn Place,
> London WC1H 0EP.

They can send you the information, but do not forget to enclose a stamped addressed envelope.

You may be interested in one or more of the books on the Books List page. Most of them are available from:

> Jewish Education Bureau
> 8 Westcombe Avenue,
> Leeds LS8 2BS.

They issue a Publications List for teachers, so perhaps your teacher can ask for a copy.

More and more schools are making visits to synagogues. Perhaps your school is one of them. Most schools come during their lesson time. Then visitors can see the various religious objects and put questions to the rabbi or other synagogue officials. An even better time to come to a synagogue is during an actual service. Many synagogues will welcome such a visit, provided, of course, they are asked in advance. There is one very important point to bear in mind. If you visit on a Sabbath or festival, please do not bring with you such items as a pen, camera, or tape recorder. By all means bring these things if your visit is on any other day.

A special word if you live in the Greater Manchester or Merseyside areas. The Centre for the Study of Religion and Education runs an urban trail on the Jewish community in Manchester. You will walk the very same streets where Jewish people lived and worked a century ago. You will see some of the original buildings used for their religious and cultural activities and have the chance to visit Jackson's Row Synagogue, or another synagogue, and eat a kosher lunch. Thousands of school children have already been on this Jewish trail. Ask your teacher to get full details from:

The Director,
Sacred Trinity Centre,
Chapel Street,
Salford M3 7AJ.

Jewish people are proud of their religion and their long history. You will not learn everything about Judaism by reading this book or even visiting a synagogue. It is hoped, however, that you are now more aware of one of the many religions found in Britain.

# Book List

D. Charing, *The Jewish World*, Macdonald 1983
A. Gilbert, *Your Neighbour Worships*, A.D.L. New York 1981
M. Levin & T. Kurzband, *The Story of the Synagogue*, Behrman,
　　　New York, 1957
S. Rossell, *When a Jew Prays*, Behrman, 1973
P. Shaw, *Visiting a Synagogue*, Board of Deputies
R. Zwerin & A. Friedman, *Our Synagogue*, Behrman 1974

In this series

S. Tompkins, *Visiting an Anglican Church*, Lutterworth
G. Palmer, *Visiting a Community Church*, Lutterworth
J. Bates, *Visiting a Methodist Church*, Lutterworth
R. Protheroe and R. Meherali, *Visiting a Mosque*, Lutterworth
D. Sullivan, *Visiting a Roman Catholic Church*, Lutterworth
M. Blackwell, *Visiting a Salvation Army Citadel*, Lutterworth
D. K. Babraa, *Visiting a Sikh Temple*, Lutterworth
D. Charing, *Visiting a Synagogue*, Lutterworth

# Glossary

*Aron Hakodesh*, the Holy Ark. The most important part of any synagogue. It houses the Torah Scrolls.

*Bar Mitzvah*, name given to a boy who reaches his thirteenth birthday and reads or chants from the Torah in front of the congregation.

*Bat Mitzvah*, similar ceremony for a girl. Often it takes place on her twelfth birthday.

*Bimah*, the raised platform in the synagogue, sometimes in the front, like a stage, whilst in other synagogues it is in the very centre facing the Ark.

*Chanukah*, a popular winter festival of lights, usually celebrated in December.

*Haftara*, the second reading from the Bible, usually from the Prophets.

*Haggadah*, a book of stories and songs about the Exodus read during the Passover seder.

*Kiddush*, reciting the blessing over wine on the eve of Sabbaths and festivals.

*Ketubah*, a Jewish marriage certificate.

*Matzot*, unleavened bread eaten by Jewish people during the festival of Passover.

*Menorah*, either the seven-branched candlestick that was found in the ancient Jewish Temple in Jerusalem, or the nine-branched one used in Jewish homes and synagogues during Chanukah.

*Mezuzah*, a little metal or wooden container and parchment scroll attached to the right hand doorpost of Jewish homes.

*Ner tamid*, the light that always burns in the synagogue.

*Orthodox*, the largest group of Jews who try to keep all the traditions, laws and customs found in the Torah and handed down from one generation to the next.

*Pesach*, the spring festival of freedom known as Passover which is usually celebrated for seven or eight days in early April.

*Purim*, a popular one day festival, usually celebrated in March and based on the Biblical book of Esther.

*Rosh Hashanah*, the Jewish New Year, usually celebrated in September.

*Seder*, the home celebration on the first, and also often on the second, evening of Passover.

*Shabbat*, the Jewish sabbath which begins on Friday evening and ends some twenty-five hours later on Saturday night.

*Shofar*, the ram's horn, blown on Rosh Hashanah and at the end of Yom Kippur.

*Sofer*, a scribe who writes Torah Scrolls and mezuzah parchments.

*Succot*, an autumn Jewish harvest festival, also known as Tabernacles. Celebrated in September or October.

*Tallit*, a prayer shawl worn by males at morning worship in both synagogues and at home.

*Yad*, the pointer used when reading from the Torah Scroll.

*Yamulkah*, skull cap used by male worshippers.

*Yom Kippur*, the Day of Atonement. A twenty-five hour fast.

# Index